Calamity Jane's Daughter: The Story of Maude Weir

A Story Never Told Before

Calamity Jane's Granddaughter
Ruth Shadley

Calamity Jane's Daughter:

The Story of Maude Weir

A Story Never Told Before

BY

Ruth Shadley

First Printing, 1996
Second Printing, 2001

Edited by James D. McLaird

Library of Congress Number 96-92330
ISBN Number 0-965271 5-0-1

Printed in the United States of America
The Caxton Printers Ltd.,Caldwell, ID

DEDICATION

Dedicated to my sister, Myrtle (who died July 7, 1995), my sister, Rose and my husband Lee who has put up with me for 35 years. "Believe me, it wasn't easy".

CONTENTS

INTRODUCTION

I know my mother was Calamity Jane's daughter, because my Dad told me she was. My sister, Rose, told me that our sister Elsie had found my mother's birth certificate in the family Bible where she knew we would find it; it stated that Calamity Jane was her mother, but my sister Elsie destroyed it. My two brothers found it out in Pierre from the neighbors. Calamity Jane tossed her last treasure, the ring the Deadwood people gave her, on my mother's bed a few days after Myrtle was born. This is the only story my mother every told us about Calamity Jane, but while she showed us the ring, she never told us why Calamity Jane gave it to her.

My mother could make a howling yodel in the back of her throat that we could hear at least a mile away, the same howl that scared away the Indians whenever Calamity Jane sat around her campfire. Last, but not least, she looked like her.

I have been reading about Calamity Jane for years trying to locate where she was in 1880 and 1884. I can find nothing; the stories are mostly the same, telling what can be found in any history book. One once in a while digs up something a little different, but not often.

My mother was Calamity Jane's daughter. I tried to find a copy of Mom's birth certificate. I sent to South Dakota, Wyoming, Nebraska, and Montana, with no luck, though I know there is one out there.

So what to do? I can't prove it, so I put off writing about what I do know. My brothers and sisters haven't told the story. Myrtle is 93, Fred died, Elsie is in a nursing home, Elmer is also dead, Rose is 82 and really doesn't care one way or the other and is busy traveling and bowling in her spare time. So its up to me if the truth is ever coming out. I'm 79 and with this traffic in Boise, Idaho, I may not have long to live.

I guess what irritates me is what people write about Calamity. My mother hated her because she was anything but a lady; she was mannish, crude, and was an ornery old drunk in her later years. She didn't like women and she made no bones about it. She liked to wear men's clothing, but who can ride horses wearing skirts? I think the stories about her being a prostitute are all wrong; she may have cooked for the Madams, but to be one of the girls, no. Can you imagine such a mannish-looking woman being cooped up in a building with a bunch of fancy looking women? She hated fancy clothes. Can you imagine a woman wearing dresses driving a freight train pulled by ten teams of oxen, snapping a bull whip to keep them going the right way? I can't.

Yes, I think she chewed tobacco and spit on the lady's fancy dress; my sister Elsie would have thought it fun, although she didn't chew tobacco, but she always liked to throw rotten tomatoes, or anything else she could come up with. One of my nieces told me that she threw half-cooked fudge on her once, just as my niece was letting her boyfriend in before going on a date.

I have never heard of Calamity killing anyone. But we all know she helped lots of people who were poorer than she was.

Sturgis, S.D., 1950, at mom and dad's 50th wedding anniversary. From left to right, back row: Myrtle, Rose, Fred, Elmer, Elsie, and Ruth. Front, seated: Maude and Will Hunt.

We all know she took care of the people in Deadwood when most of them had smallpox. We all know she could shoot straight. My whole family took after her on that; wc were all taught how to handle a gun and most of us are dead shots. My little brother Elmer was a sharp-shooter and had a medal for it.

Photo of Maude Weir

Maude Weir with daughter Myrtle

Maude Weir

Photo Courtesy of The Montana Historical Society

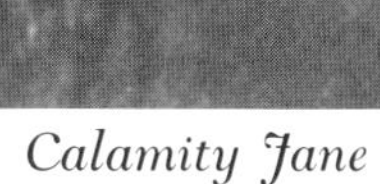

Calamity Jane

Photo Courtesy of The Montana Historical Society

Calamity Jane

Compare these three photographs of Maude Weir, left, with the two pictures of Calamity Jane, right.

Calamity could ride a horse where most people couldn't drag the halter, which was my Dad's favorite saying. No she didn't ride around barrels; she rode over mountains and up rivers in the cold and snow where nobody else could get through. As we all know, she was a scout and a stage driver. Most of the books I've read told about all of her bad traits, except Zack Sutley who wrote The Last Frontier. He has a chapter in his book in which he tells about the hardships the oxen drivers had to put up with while driving freight trains from Fort Pierre to Deadwood. Can you imagine any woman of today that would get off welfare long enough to drive an ox team?

Yes, I know Calamity had one daughter, or maybe even two, born out of wedlock, probably conceived under a bush, but as I look into today's paper, I see two girls who have babies out of wedlock, and tomorrow there will probably be two or three more, yet it was a crime when Calamity had one.

She had no childbirth protection, no welfare to turn to, no family to go to, no grandmother to take care of the baby while she went to the mall. No, she took care of my mother for almost two years all by herself, probably in an old shack that had no electricity, no water in the house, and the only heat that came from a small stove or maybe a bonfire. Yes, I imagine she shot game and all kinds of birds, but there was no law against that. When she got desperate she took her baby to its father and asked him to care for it as she knew it would have a good life with him.

People thought she was a terrible woman because she got drunk. There was no A.A. then. She like to drink with men as she liked to drink in saloons where the action was, not like the other women of her time who drank behind closed doors and tearfully waited at home for their husbands who were having fun in the town's saloons, dancing with the saloon gals.

No, I don't believe Calamity married Wild Bill Hickok. I read several books about him, some good and some bad, but even it she did, my mother was born in 1881, years after Hickok was killed. I think she would have liked to have married him as she thought he was great, but I'm glad he isn't my grandfather, even if he was thought of as a great shot. Some say he was a man to shoot without hesitation and kill anyone that he knew he could outshoot, but of course this also came out of books.

Yes, I believe Calamity married Clinton Burke of Texas in 1885. He may have had a daughter by a former wife, but it was not my mother as she was born in 1881. Some of the books said Calamity was married to a dozen men. The only one of them that sounds familiar to me is Hunt. My mother, Maude, was married to him, not Calamity; that's how history gets all mixed up.

Then there was a woman named Janey, the one that had all of those letters from Calamity and who insisted she was Calamity's daughter. When the newspapers came out telling about her in 1941, we were in Wallace, Idaho, where my husband was working for the Hecla Mining Company. I was working in a beauty shop. I didn't know how Mom would take it, so my husband told me to go home and help her if I could. Mom didn't know that I knew who she was. When I got home, nobody mentioned it until the news came on the radio. Mom listened a few moments, then she shut off the radio and said, "that woman is a dirty liar and she is trying to fool the government to get money." Then she looked at me and shut up. Dad gave me a look to not say anything, so I didn't. I stayed a few more days, but nobody mentioned it again. I've read the letters and copied them. They sound as if Calamity may have written them, but we also know she liked to make up stories as she sat alone by her campfire, probably half drunk, trying to make up a life she would have liked to have had.

Mom had several pictures of Calamity with her favorite horse, Satan, that she kept in an old trunk. None of us ever asked her where she got them or why she kept them. After all of us left home most of these pictures disappeared, as only a few were in her papers. One of the pictures Mom kept was a picture of Calamity all dressed up in fancy buckskins when she was with Buffalo Bill's Wild West Show, where she rode standing up in the saddle shooting at her hat as she circled the ring. It was a shame when she got too drunk to do her act and Buffalo Bill had to fire her; he lost a real artist and she lost all hope of being what she had always wanted to be, a dream she dreamed about so often.

I wish that she hadn't been a drunk. I wish she could have been someone we could all have been real proud of, especially my mother who always tried to keep the truth from us all. She didn't want us ashamed of her; of course, none of us are. She was one of the world's best mothers and I hope if she is looking down on me, she will forgive me and understand why I had to let history know the truth, as I am proud of them both.

Calamity Jane's Daughter:
The Story of Maude Weir

A Story Never Told Before

Maude Myrtle Weir Hunt, Age 12 years, ll months, Pierre South Dakota, 1893.

The Story of Maude Weir

I like to imagine that this is the way Calamity Jane gave her daughter, Maude, up for adoption:

> *It was a cold day in September 1883 when a woman wearing buckskins and a large brown hat strolled into Long Jo's saloon in Pierre, S.D. It was a new building, a white clapboard, with large oak timbers upon a rock foundation, with living quarters on the second floor; it also had many bedrooms. The saloon itself was on one end, with an adjoining large dining room, with several large tables; beyond the dining room was another large room where the cowboys could dance the night away. A large grand piano graced the center; an old violin lay upon its shiny surface. Long Jo himself played this beautiful sounding instrument, whether it was a waltz, square dancing, or just a hoedown. He played them all. Joe watched the buckskin-covered lady as she came through the door; although he was behind the bar serving drinks, he wondered what she was pulling through the door on a small rope. Nobody, including himself, had seen this figure for about two-and-a-half years. The woman waved a gloved hand as she pulled on the rope; on the end of the rope a small child almost two years old*

stumbled through the door. Nobody could see if it was a boy or a girl as the tangled hair almost covered her tiny face. An oversized coat covered most of its body; the sleeves were rolled up and two tiny hands wiggled out. A grizzled old man waved from one of the tables, "Come on and have a drink, Calamity. We haven't seen you for a long time; you must be awfully dry." "I will later on," replied Calamity, "but I need to talk to Jo first." Long Jo waved Calamity into a small room behind the bar. Calamity herded the small child into the small room. "Well Jo, I'm at the end of my rope; with winter coming on I can't take my kid along when I'm freighting and the company said I could have my old job back between here and Deadwood, so as it's your kid too, I thought maybe you could take care of her; it's just too tough a life with me. As you haven't any kids, this one won't do any harm." Long Jo smiled as the little girl stretched out her little hand to him. "My wife has always wanted a kid but I don't think she would consider yours. You know how she hates you." "Well, what she don't know won't hurt her," replied Calamity. "You can tell her it's somebody else's such as Sadie Beck's. She is always having kids; I'm sure she would say it's hers. I've helped her out a lot of times; she is about the only woman friend I have. I sure wish you would take her Jo, as you know I like my whiskey. We darn near died last winter. I want to leave her with somebody that will give her the life she deserves. I'll let you adopt her so all will be legal. I'd like to see her once in a while, but I promise you I won't cause you any trouble, or tell her I'm her mother. I just need a home for her." Long Jo sat in deep thought as he stroked his beard, then he called Jenny, his Negro house keeper.

"Jenny, take this child upstairs and clean her up and get some decent clothes on her, then I'll take her in to see Mary.

This is what happened to Calamity Jane's daughter, the daughter everyone has wondered about. On September 10, 1883, Jo and Mary Weir adopted Myrtle Maude, the real daughter of Calamity Jane. They decided to call her Maude Myrtle instead of Myrtle Maude.

Maude Weir, about three years old, taken from an old tin type

Dad's prize team that he cut the speltz with while mom and I watched

Maude Weir Hunt making soap on the farm, about 1921

It was an uphill climb for Mrs. Weir. Here was a small child looking for the life it needed, and here was a woman who never had a child and she didn't know what to do. Jenny took over the child's needs and to Joe the child was perfect and he showed t. The child soon knew who loved her and who didn't. Mary was left out and she was a fragile person whom Joe adored, so what to do? As the months slipped by, it was clear something had to be done. Calamity always came into the saloon whenever the freight wagons came by, but she never interfered. Joe knew something had to be done as his wife seemed depressed, so he asked Calamity what he could do as he didn't want to lose the child or his wife and it seemed they would never get along.

He heard of a place that took in children. It was a Catholic academy called St. Martin's, located near Sturgis up near Deadwood. They took in kids without a home, and it was also a school, which Pierre didn't have. Joe decided to write to the Academy and he found they would take the girl, but they needed someone to bring her to Sturgis.

Calamity volunteered to take Maude to the Academy on the stage coach. This she did. Maude's life at the Academy was a happy life; other children were there to play with, and the nuns were very nice. They taught her many things, such as manners, to dress neatly, and to brush her dark hair until it shone.

Maude missed her Father Weir, as she always called him. He wrote her many letters. The nuns always read them to her, until they taught her to read them herself.

Calamity Jane would sometimes stop in to see Maude, but Maude always hated it, although she didn't know she was her

Territory of Dakota
County of Hughes

In the Probate Court
of said County Before
C D Mead Esquire
Probate Judge

In the Matter of the Adoption of Maude Beck an infant } Order

On this 10th day of
September A.D. 1883 personally
appeared before C.D. Mead
Probate Judge in and for said
County, Sadie Beck Joseph
W. Weir and Mary H Weir his
wife, and it appearing to me
that the said Sadie Beck
is the mother of an infant
named Maude Beck aged
22 months, and born ~~out~~ of
lawful wedlock . is willing
to consent to the adoption of
said infant ~~infant~~ by said
Joseph W Weir and Mary
H. Weir, and the said
Joseph W Weir and Mary H Weir
are willing to adopt the

Maude's adoption papers, September 10, 1883

said infant - and the said Sadie Beck having by the agreement herein filed consented to said adoption in writing signed by her, and the said Joseph W Weir and Mary H. Weir having signed and executed said agreement whereby they agree that said Child shall be adopted by them and treated in all respects as their own lawful Child should be treated.

And the said Sadie Beck Joseph W Weir and Mary H. Weir being each seperately examined by me and it appearing to me that the interests of such Child will be promoted by such adoption, Ordered that said adoption be and the same is hereby approved, and that said Child shall hence forth be regarded and treated in all respects as the Child of the said Joseph W. Weir and Mary H Weir

C. D. Mead
Probate Judge

Joseph Weir and Maude Weir, 1899. Maude was 18 years old.

mother. Calamity was always dirty from driving the freighters and sometimes drunk, so Maude was ashamed of her. She couldn't understand why a person like her would come and see her, and Calamity didn't tell her.

Maude loved to read and write; she wrote such a beautiful hand. She also liked geography class; they had such fun seeing who could name the states, all world countries, and the capitals of each. The nuns made most studies a game.

Then life changed for Maude. Joe Weir brought his daughter home to Pierre. Everything seemed so different, but her father Weir was there and Negro Jenny was always there to help. They both loved her.

This was in 1895, and Maude was fourteen years of age, and Pierre now had a school. Joe was so proud of his almost-grown daughter, he hired a dressmaker to make sure she looked proper. Her stepmother treated her well although she seemed more fragile.

Maude went to the new school, but it was very different. The kids were all strangers, but she had a good teacher, Anne M. Bailey. She put Maude in the fourth grade to start, and before the term was out, she promoted her to the fifth grade, as she had an average of 98%. The subjects were reading, spelling, writing, language, geography, and arithmetic.

Maude's stepmother died on February 15, 1895, and Joe had more time for his daughter. He bought her a small horse and let her ride; when she learned that, he got her a small buggy and taught her how to drive. This she really liked as all the town's ladies drove buggies. Of course, Calamity didn't like it as it was too fancy and she said so on one of her trips to Pierre. She thought Joe was making a sissy out of her.

Long Jo's saloon in Pierre, South Dakota, which later became the Weir family home.

Then word got out that Maude was Calamity Jane's daughter. Whether it was Calamity's fault or not nobody seems to know. She may have hollered it to the house tops while she was roaring drunk, or she was just trying to stir up some excitement, but a small number of people knew about it. Dr. Hoyt knew it, and he was always there whenever Maude was sick. When Maude found out about it, she was shocked. What had she done to deserve this? She wanted to run away and hide her head; what would people think of her? To think that she was the daughter of such an old drunk; she thought the world around her had collapsed. She grew into herself and stayed in her room.

Finally Father Weir talked to her and asked her what she would like to do. She told him she would like to learn to play

PIERRE PUBLIC SCHOOLS.

Report of Maud Weir

Member of Fourth Grade.

Anna M. Bailey
TEACHER.

	1st 6 w.	2d 6 w.	3d 6 w.	4th 6 w.	5th 6 w.	6th 6 w.	Year Avr.
Days Taught	30	28	29		37	50	
Days Present	29½	28	28½		34½	50	
Days Absent	½	0	½		4½	0	
Times Tardy	0	0	0		0	0	
Reading	98	98	98		97	99	
Spelling	98	100	100		96	96	
Writing	98	98	98		98	98	
Language and Grammar	98	99	98		90	100	
Geography	100	100	98		98	99	
Arithmetic	100	99	99		94	97	
U. S. History							
Physiology							
Civil Government							
Literature							
Rhetoric							
English History							
General History							
Algebra							
Geometry							
Physics							
Political Economy							
Botany							
Geology							
Astronomy							
Deportment	100	100	99		100	100	
Rank in Class	1	1	1		2		2
Pupils in Class	18	18	17		14	14	
Average Standing	98⅔	99	98½		95⅚	98½	98

Certificate of Promotion

Standing 98

Rank 2

Promoted to Fifth Grade

DATED

June 8 1894.

Seventy-five per cent. average necessary to continue in Grade.

SIGNATURE OF PARENTS.

Joseph W. Weir
Joseph White Weir
Joseph White Weir
J. W. Weir

Maude Weir's report card from Pierre Public School

the piano so she could accompany him when he played the violin. She also wanted him to make sure Calamity stayed away from her. This he agreed to do. He taught her all the songs, including all the words; she had a good voice and could memorize about anything. While practicing one day, she found out she had an unusual sound in the back of her throat that can only be described as a sort of a howl or a wail that could be heard for a mile. She used this many years later to locate some of her children. Her father knew where she got the trill or howl, but he didn't mention it. Calamity was noted for it; she used it to scare away the Indians when they got too close. They couldn't imagine how a white woman could out howl them; they didn't as a rule bother her and they called her the devil of the white spirit.

The years went by and Maude found out most friends stayed by her, the ones that lived in the small neighborhood; she didn't stray far and she kept to herself alot. Then one day a tall stranger came by; he had almost black hair, with a gold-colored mustache, his hips were thin and his shoulders were broad, and he had long fingers on a firm hand. He was just a stray, cleaner than most, and he had beautiful blue eyes that smiled, although the lips stayed motionless. Maude took one look at him and was very well pleased with what she saw. She had her father introduce them although her father thought he was too old a man for his daughter. Later they found he was eleven years her senior, but a young girl in love has no reason he found out. The man's name was Fred William Hunt. He had been raised on a farm in the state of Michigan and had several sisters and one living brother, Frank.

CERTIFIED COPY OF MARRIAGE LICENSE.

No. 407.

THE STATE OF SOUTH DAKOTA } ss
COUNTY OF HUGHES

IN THE CIRCUIT COURT
Sixth Judicial Circuit

To any Person Lawfully Authorized to Solemnize Marriage in Said State:

KNOW YE, That License is hereby granted to join together as

HUSBAND AND WIFE

Fred William Hunt of the City of Pierre County of Hughes State of S.D. and Myrtle Maud Weir of the City of Pierre County of Hughes State of S.D. I, James W. Morse Clerk of the Circuit Court in and for the County of Hughes and State of South Dakota, being satisfied ~~from the affidavit of~~ ~~and~~ that there are no legal impediments to the consummation of said marriage

Therefore, *this shall be your sufficient authority for solemnizing the marriage of said parties and making due return thereof as provided by law.*

In Testimony Whereof, *I have hereunto set my hand and affixed the seal of this court, this 25th ~~of December 1900~~.*

James W. Morse
Clerk of the Circuit Court.

[SEAL.] *By ____ Deputy.*

I William A. Lyman a Minister of the Gospel and a resident of the City of Pierre County of Hughes and State of South Dakota, do hereby certify and return that on the 25th day of December in the year of our Lord One Thousand ~~Eight~~ Nine Hundred ~~and Ninety~~ I did join together in the Bonds of Holy Matrimony according to the laws of the State of South Dakota Fred William Hunt and Myrtle Maud Weir they being known to me to be the same persons named in the foregoing license, and I further certify and return that said marriage ceremony was performed in the presence of the persons who have subscribed their names hereto.

In Presence of

Joseph White Weir
I Reside in Pierre
J. B. Repine
I Reside in Pierre

William A. Lyman
Pastor Cong'l Church
Fred W. Hunt Husband
M. M. Weir Hunt Wife.

The State of South Dakota, } ss
County of Hughes.

I, James W. Morse Clerk of the Circuit Court, Sixth Judicial Circuit, County of Hughes, State of South Dakota, being a Court of Record, do hereby certify that I have carefully compared the above Marriage License and Certificate with the original License and Certificate of Marriage of Fred William Hunt and Myrtle Maud Weir and find the same to be a true and correct transcript thereof as the same appears on file and of record in the Clerk's office of said Circuit Court at the City of Pierre, in said County of Hughes.

WITNESS my hand and the seal of said Circuit Court the 25th day of May 1901.

James W. Morse
Clerk of the Circuit Court.
By ____ Deputy

My mother's marriage license

Fred William Hunt was usually called Will. He had eased his way west working wherever he could. He even raced in the opening of the Cherokee strip, where he got a piece of land from the government. The wagons and horses lined up and when the gun went off everybody shot into action; most of them knew where they wanted to go so the race was on. Whoever got to the place they wanted, they stopped and staked it out. Will found a piece of land he liked and staked it out, but he sold it out to a man who had a plow and a few head of stock; as Will didn't have anything to start with, he decided to sell it. He then rode on to work on farms and ranches. One time he worked for a man who had a car, or auto as they called them then. He was interested in it and the farmer let him drive it a few times. He was fascinated with how it worked, but that winter he moved on and got a job on the railroad which was also interesting. His job was a brakeman, but his dream was to be the engineer; to be one, he had to have more education than he had. He had only three years of grade school; he could read and write some, and did all his figuring as he called it in his head, and he was very good at that. His German father, who had changed his real last name from Hundt to Hunt when he came to the U.S.A., didn't believe in school; he said school was just for the rich kids. His father was a mean old German who made all of his children go to church on Sunday morning, then beat his Irish wife and children in the afternoon. All the children left or ran away from home as soon as they could; none of them ever knew when he died or where he was buried, and none of them cared.

Will got a job as the first Taxi driver in Pierre; shortly afterwards he married Maude on Christmas Day, 1900. Pastor

William A. Lyman of the Congregational Church performed the wedding. Joe Weir insisted the newly wed couple move in with him as the place was large and he didn't want his daughter to move away where he couldn't see her. He still had Jenny to do most of the house work and he wanted her to show Maude how to cook.

Will learned more about autos and how to repair them. Meanwhile, his family grew. A daughter was born to them October 17, 1901, a small-boned beautiful girl with dark hair and brown eyes like her mother. Dr. Hoyt was there for her. A few days after the birth of her daughter, Maude was surprised to see Calamity Jane striding up the street. Calamity hadn't bothered her for a long time, but when she heard Maude had a baby daughter, she just had to see her. Will let her come in as he saw for a change that Calamity was dressed in clean buckskins and she wasn't drunk.

Calamity went to the bed and looked down at her daughter and the new baby granddaughter: "what a beautiful baby, she is almost as beautiful as her mother." Maude just looked at her and said, "I wish you would go and not come back." Tears came to Calamity's eyes as she slipped a gold ring off her finger and tossed it onto the bed: "the people of Deadwood gave me this ring and it is the only thing I have left to give. I don't feel young anymore, so I better give this to you in case you will need it to raise your Brat. You're my only daughter." With that she strode out the door. She never came back.

The next spring Joseph Weir died (April 1902). This was hard on Maude, but as she was the only heir, she inherited everything, including the saloon which was closed; it gave Maude and her family a place to live, which they needed as

Maude had another child. This time it was a blue-eyed boy with black hair. Father Weir also left a lot of nice furniture: the large piano and a nice dresser with a large mirror and a beautiful marble base. There also were many guns; a 45-90 was the rarest. It was a rifle with engraved cartage in silver; its stock was a highly polished wood. Maude learned later that there were only three made. There were also several old flintlock pistols and a small gun that Wild Bill Hickok gave to Mrs. Weir when he bought a pair of pistols. He gave it to her and told her if she ever shot at any one with it and missed, he hoped it would explode and kill her; she never shot it. There was also a roulette wheel that could be controlled under the table with a well-placed foot. And there was a gold watch and a large gold nugget that hung down off a gold chain, a beautiful thing, and a pewter snuff box which is all engraved, and several gold coins.

The next child Maude and Will had was a couple years later. She was different in many ways as she had light curly hair and mischievous blue eyes. How she loved to shake those beautiful curls and giggle. Of course, everybody talked to her and left the older two to watch and get jealous. Elsie is what they named her. You might say she was another Calamity Jane, and as she grew so did her temperament. He mother paddled her little butt but nothing seemed to help; she couldn't get along with her sister or brother, or anyone else for that matter.

Will always had a job, working at the water station to keep the electric motors running, and his family kept growing. They had another boy; he was also light-haired with blue eyes, and was the smallest, a good-natured boy who loved to play with nuts and bolts by himself if only Elsie would leave him alone. Myrtle would try to protect the little boy, whom they called Elmer, but Elsie would tease him whenever she couldn't find anything else to do.

Five years later Maude had another dark-haired girl. Maude had a miscarriage two years before, which almost cost her life, but Dr. Hoyt pulled her through. Rose, as they called the new baby, was more like Myrtle, and Elsie didn't seem to tease her as much. The rest of the kids could be playing peacefully, but when Elsie showed up, everything seemed to explode. She was stronger than all the rest, and was the town bully; she could outswim them all. They had the Missouri River close by, and they swam in a bay.

Three years later, Maude had another dark-haired girl, whom they called Ruth. She had brown eyes and had wavy hair, but not as curly as Elsie's. She was the last one of this family, and was shy and didn't like people, a hermit like her famous Grandmother.

Sadie Beck

Sadie Beck, the woman who signed the adoption papers for Calamity Jane, worked as a cook around Pierre for several years. Some say she left Pierre and married an English Lord or Earl. The marriage didn't last; she may have divorced him, or he may have died. I believe she was Calamity Jane's sister. She had a child who was about Maude's age who died shortly after Maude was adopted. She tried to get Joseph Weir to give her Maude, as she was all alone; this Joseph Weir would not do He said he couldn't part with Maude. After Joseph Weir died, Sadie Beck helped Maude and told people she was Maude's mother. This Maude agreed to do as she didn't want any more people to learn she was Calamity's daughter. Any body was better than Calamity, and after all Sadie's name was on Maude's adoption papers. This is why most people couldn't find Calamity's daughter after some of the old timers died and after Maude and her family moved to the Black Hills.

Sadie Beck married Jack Parker. He was a small man who didn't like work. Maude had a few dollars, so Sadie and Maude bought a farm near Sturgis, S.D. Sadie had changed her name from Sadie to Sarah so she was known as Sarah Parker. The farm was located in a community known as Upper Alkali. Sarah and Jack Parker moved onto the farm; Sarah did most of the work, with some help from a man named Charlie. Together they build a sandstone barn; it was a huge barn with a large granary at one end. Many horses kept warm when the winter winds blew. They also planted many trees, apple and cottonwood. Sarah wrote to Maude often and wanted Maude to move as soon as possible as Jack was mean to her and her health was failing, but Maude was pregnant with Ruth and was in no condition to move. Finally, Ruth Sarah (named after her so-called Grandmother) was born July 15, 1915. Maude then received word that Sarah died on July 19, 1915. Word was also that the farm they bought together was not Maude's anymore, as Jack Parker owned it all. Maude insisted she still wanted to move to the Black Hills, as Pierre was growing fast and Elsie was becoming a problem living in town. She thought perhaps the country would be good for her, and the rest of the family as well, so three months later they packed their things in a freight train, including a black horse that Will liked and a two-year-old heifer.

It was hard for Maude to leave the old place, but her children's welfare came first, and people in the Black Hills didn't known she was Calamity's daughter. She would be able to hold her head high as Sarah was respected there as a hard-working farmer. All went well and Jack Parker told them they could stay with him for awhile as he needed help and knew Will had lived on a farm when he was a kid. This we did, but the kids got on Jack's nerves, so they decided to move to a vacant farm a few miles east. They stayed there for three years; the farm wasn't near as good as the one Parker had; he didn't farm it or take care of it or the livestock, so Will decided to try and raise enough money to buy it. An older man who lived a few miles south said he would loan Will the money and he could repay it every year at harvest time until it was paid off.

The trees Sarah had planted were growing; the big barn was nice and the house was much nicer than the one they had been living in. Of course, there was no electricity or bathroom, but there was lots of water. There were several wells that had lots of water as cold as ice, and a small creek ran down through most of the land where cattle, horses, and all the chickens and ducks could drink.

This is the farm I loved and lived on as I am the youngest child they called Ruth.

Ruth's Childhood

The world looked bright for all of us. We had a nice farm with all the needed machinery, with all of us working together. We were all given jobs that we liked the best. My little brother Elmer chopped the wood, and he had the worst job of all and that was being the one who was on top of the hay stack on hot July days, but he liked to lay the hay as perfectly as was possible so the wind and rain didn't get in and rot the hay. We thought he was the best in the community. My sister Elsie was a great cook; she liked that as she didn't like to get her fingers dirty. She loved to cook and to play any instrument that she could get her fingers on. Rose liked the chickens, ducks, turkeys, and geese, but her main chore was to keep me out of trouble. She made little coops where we put the old hens that had baby chicks. Of course she helped milk the cow's night and morning, like we all did while Mom cooked breakfast and a light supper.

I was the youngest and everybody bossed me and dragged me out of lots of fun; it was so good to get away from them as I hated to be bossed. When I got old enough, I'd climb on a horse and take off. Rose always had to go with me until I was about five. Dad insisted I could ride good enough to go by myself to get the cows which we put in eighty acres; that was down the road, but I had to ride the old reliable horse, the one they had brought from Pierre. Of course, I had to do my own saddling or I wasn't allowed to go. Dad had covered the stirrups of onc of the saddles and I had to use it. I'd tie the horse to the manger, then climb up on the manger after I had boosted the saddle up on the manger. It took a while, but while I was doing that I kept out of trouble. When that was accomplished, I could go after the cows by myself. They learned that I was the cowgirl, which came in handy when the drought descended on South Dakota along with the millions of grasshoppers that was the start of the depression. The land dried up as there was no rain or snow in the winter time; our creeks dried up, and the wells had to be dug deeper.

I remember a time when Dad was out binding a small acreage that had speltz growing on it, which we used for horse grain and chicken feed. There was a wild-looking cloud forming in the west. I had always been scared of lightning, so I stood as close as I could to Mom as she watched it out of the living room window. It was coming closer and closer. We could see Dad as he was trotting his prize team, which he never did as a rule. The storm came on faster and faster. Mom stood there praying that there was no hail in the storm, but we could see it had white streaks in it, and it was coming right over the field where my Dad was trying to get as much cut down as he could. The lightning started full force, and although there was a small acreage left, Dad had to bring his horses in and unhook them before the hail started. He got them inside the large barn before the hail really began. The uncut grain was ruined, but that cut and lying on the ground was saved. Some was beat out but he saved most of it. Mom believed it was Dad's good driving, but I always thought it was Mom's praying.

The first thing I remember was when I was about two years old, and we lived at the first farm. I remember there was about a nine inch step that went into the bedrooms; of course, I fell the first few times I tried it without help. I never did like somebody helping me or telling me what I could or could not do (and still don't), but I do remember the first time I crawled down that step by myself.

I also remember the time when we lived at this farm when a large flock of wild geese flew over and circled overhead; Mom was home with just us kids, but she grabbed up the 45-90 and ran out on the porch that was just off the kitchen which was about two feet off the ground, with steps at one side. We all watched as Mom took aim at the large birds. She squatted down close to one edge and fired away; the gun went off with a terrible roar. We all watched as Mom was knocked off the porch. She got up unhurt and said, "don't any of you kids ever fire this gun as it kicks like Hell."

After we moved to the other farm, everything was fun. We had a dog, lots of cats, cows and calves, chickens, ducks, geese, turkeys, and best of all, lots of horses and a team of mules. I loved horses, and it didn't make any difference whether it was the large mules or the smaller saddle horses. I loved them all.

Mom always had a large garden. She had a green thumb if anybody ever did. Dad would plow the garden for her, and cultivate it when the weeds got too thick. We sold the surplus to the grocery store in Sturgis, but she usually canned most of it, so we had vegetables all winter long. She also canned beef whenever Dad butchered a calf or hog.

We lived in a small community. The farm was about 365 acres. The neighbors were all friendly. We had lots of picnics and the card games were great; we had several tables and everyone played. There was a prize for the highest; nothing very expensive, but usually funny. At the picnics, the men and boys played baseball while the rest cheered them on. After the ball game they had the picnic, which was really something. It seemed the women were the best cooks and everybody brought whatever they thought was the best. Mom always brought ice cream made with real cream and eggs; we all had to help turn the freezer, while another filled in more ice. It was always a fun thing and the taste was just out of this world. Another lady could make the best banana cream pie; we always asked for a piece of hers until one day us girls sneaked up behind a tree to watch her put in the bananas. After she put the filling in the crust, she sliced the bananas on top; then she pushed them down with a finger and licked off her finger before she pushed down another one. We thought that was awful as our mothers didn't do it that way; ours always taught us never to lick off our fingers and put them back in the food. We all let the adults eat that pie that day.

We had a one room school house. We were lucky as we lived only a quarter of a mile from it; some of the other kids had to walk about three miles. In the wintertime this was bad as South Dakota is noted for its blizzards, but they seldom missed a day. As a rule we had the best of teachers and some stayed several years. The one that stands out to me was Alice Hale. I believe she taught us more in the years she put up with us that any other teacher. The teachers of today think they are overloaded with work if they have twenty pupils, but all are in the same grade. Our teachers as a rule had twenty pupils in eight grades. She taught every subject in very grade. Just stop and think what that meant: every grade and all the subjects in each grade. We had reading, writing, arithmetic, spelling, hygiene, civics, geography, drawing, and English, along with singing. We had a recess mid-morning and mid-afternoon. We started at 9 o'clock and stayed until four o'clock. We also had a noon hour, so we could run off our energy playing baseball or tag of some kind. Some would have arguments but it never came to blows; if it got a little rough, the teacher came out to see what was going on. If she could decide who was to blame, we all had to go in and take our seats. Nobody wanted to go in, so there weren't many fights. when we went to a high school in town, we were usually ahead of the kids who went to town school.

When we got home from school, we did our chores, which were feeding the livestock and milking the cows. We had about twenty-five cows and we all helped Dad while Mom got supper. Everybody helped. We would have a squabble once in a while, but Mom would sometimes just look at us and if that didn't work, a good swat on the rear end helped. Dad I don't think every swatted any of us; he left it to my mother, which I always thought she enjoyed. Anyway, I always thought she looked like she was enjoying it. I was my Daddy's darling. I always got my share or maybe I was like my grandmother and needed it more often.

Whenever we needed help, Mom was always there. I remember the many times she would run out of the house and grab a hoe that was always kept near the kitchen door, whenever some of us hollered snake. We always had a few rattlers. Our dog was bitten one time as he grabbed one before Mom got there. The snakes didn't have a chance with Mom and here deadly hoe. The dog survived as Mom stayed up most of the night pouring kerosene on the wound, and she pulled him through.

The hundreds of times when I woke up not being able to breathe as I always had the croup (any way that's what people called it then), she would sit for hours in her rocking chair beside my bed putting everything you can imagine on my throat, from skunk oil and goose grease to mustard plaster. How I hated that, but we never argued with my mother. Whenever she got me to breathing again normally, she would sing me songs in a low voice so as not to awaken the others. She knew hundreds of songs. One that I liked was "In the Baggage Coach Ahead." It had such a pretty tune; I would doze off to sleep, and she would go back to bed until I had another attack.

The good times outnumbered the bad times. There was always fun somewhere even if it was work. I was allowed to help Elmer shingle the roof of the big barn which was steep; every shingle had to placed in a certain place. I liked helping my brother whom I adored. He would wrestle with Rose and I, but never hurt us, and I know sometimes we hurt him when both of us would pile on him, and we weren't a fragile pair.

We had great neighbors. There were two families of Matz's, the Nelsons, the Hoopers, the Gilberts, the Ahrendsons, the Sutters, the Torrences, and a couple families of Grubles. Pete and family lived on the old farm first; he could play most anything, the violin, mouth harp, and the bones. He and his family would come up to our place as we had a very large kitchen; it was a great place to dance. He taught us all how to square dance; he could play and guide us through the maze of steps. I was only about six, but he said I could learn too. Mom would join in and Dad would stand in the doorway, watching and enjoying every minute of it. When he found out that Mom had a violin, he tuned it and was real surprised to hear the beautiful sound that came out. Elsie was fascinated with it, so Pete told Elsie he would teach her to play it, but he didn't know much about reading notes as he played by ear. She didn't care how she played it, just as long as she could learn to play tunes the way he did. He taught her how to tune it and where to put her fingers to make the different sounds. That was all it took; she learned to master it in no time. Pete and his wife moved to another farm, but before they left his wife taught Mom how to crochet, which she really enjoyed.

THE GREAT DEPRESSION

I really don't remember how many years the depression lasted, but it seemed endless. Nobody liked it, and nobody had any money. We did things that didn't cost anything, such as playing cards. The whole neighborhood took part. We had to sell most of our cows as we had no feed for them. I remember the government would give us twenty dollars a head for each cow if we could get them to Sturgis on a certain day. The cows were worth much more, but it was better than having them starve right before our eyes.

A captain at Fort Meade had sold me a small horse a few years before, as his nine-year-old was afraid of it. It was small, but a horse that could travel for miles without rest. When word got out that we had to get the cows there by night, a neighbor and Dad decided to take in ours and his that morning. We had a few saddle horses left. We got our cows in O.K., but when the neighbor and I got back, Dad told us that another neighbor needed his cows taken in, and he didn't have any horses left. We had one fresh horse, but only one, so my small horse had to go. Dad said, "he can make it Ruth, but please don't race him back this time." I hadn't realized that Dad knew we had raced all the way home on the first trip as we had walked our horses when we got close to home. Dad just knew.

The depression made an impression on all of us. It taught us to watch every dime. I herded the cattle into every fence corner, around the fields and roads that might produce a stray mouthful. It seemed like every time a spear of grass ventured out of the ground a dozen grasshoppers were waiting for its arrival. I so hated them. One time I snapped my cattle whip around a fence post and I counted over 50 hoppers. The hoppers would go to the fence posts for shade from the blistering sun, then follow around the post as they earth followed around the sun.

My horse, dog, and myself did the same thing around a small hay stack. We all looked forward to the winter time as it might produce some snow. Of course, the wind usually blew it up in high piles. We were glad we lived in the western part of South Dakota instead of the eastern part as their land was more prairie, and we had mountains nearby. But most of all there was always hope that it would be like it was years before, when the streams stretched almost across the entire farm. It was very sad, but most of the time the winters were not good, with the blowing snow and below zero temperature, but it was better than the blowing dirt that covered our fences. We would dig out, but there was always another wind. The only good thing about the wind was it furnished us with power to run our radio. Dad took a generator, put a blade on it that he had carefully made out of a piece of wood. There was a wire leading down a long pole which he had put in the ground; he hooked this to an old A battery that ran our radio. The radio took several other batteries which had to be replaced about every year, if we didn't play it too much, but the A battery was the main power. The blade was balanced so it would spin with a light wind, and wind we had plenty of. My Mother's favorite program was Amos and Andy; she would laugh until tears came. After the program she would go out and look up at the stars. She could name most of the big ones; she would point them out to us. Of course, we liked the big dipper the best, and I liked the milky way with all those stars blending into one mass; they were all so beautiful, especially on a cold winter night. To me, that was living. Mom also liked the moon. She would point out the face and told us there was a man in the moon. She would look up at it and say, someday we will be able to fly to the moon, then we can see what that man really looks like. I sure wished she could of been living when they landed on the moon.

Family Stories

Myrtle wasn't home much as I was growing up; she went to normal school as soon as she could as she wanted to teach school. She became a one-room school teacher for several years. Then she married Emmette Quatier. Fred, the oldest boy, also married the same year, so that just left the four of us at home: Elsie, Elmer, Rose, and myself.

A funny thing happened the day Fred was married. I'll never forget. We had gotten up early. We had milked the cows and had the separating done before we went to dress for the wedding. The wedding was at Fred's wife's home; she lived with her folks on a farm about ten miles from us. It was in December and like South Dakota usually is, it was cold and of course the wind blew. Dad had dressed and went out to hook up his best team, which was a pair of big beautiful sorrel mares, to a wagon that he had filled with straw and blankets. Everything was going along fine; everyone had on their best clothes, and Mom was fixing her hair. We had a large mirror that hung just behind the separator. Rose was combing her hair, looking into the mirror, a large pail of separated milk on one of the separator stools which could be moved so the milk would go into the pail. Anyway, as Rose swirled around she bumped into the pail and down it came, spilling the milk all over the kitchen floor. My mother came out to see what had happened this time; she took one look at the milk and jumped up and down, saying "Shit-Shit-Shit." I put my hand over my mouth and ran out of the room, as Mom didn't get mad very often, but when she did, it was best to get out of the way. My Dad came in at that time to tell us he was ready; he helped Mom clean the mess up, but days afterwards he would tell about it and laugh about it till the tears ran down his cheeks.

Maude, or Mom as I knew her, never talked about her life when she was a kid, but she had one enemy, and that was Dad's brother, Frank. He'd blow in like he was king. My mother always warned us to keep away from him as he was a bad man, not like our Dad. Of course, we asked why, and she told us he had been in prison several times, and to just stay away from him, but as he was Dad's brother, not to be mean to him. She said he was a liar and not to believe anything he said. She promised to get him out as soon as possible.

Uncle Frank was a ornery man and loved to tease Mom. One day as we were eating dinner, he asked Mom if she had ever told us who her real mother was. A hush fell over the table, and Dad spoke up and told Frank to shut up or get out. Frank was smart as he knew Dad wasn't fooling, so he said no more, but waited until Dad was out in one of the fields, then he came around to where Rose and I were and told us Mom was Calamity Jane's daughter and that all the people in Pierre knew it. Rose always tried to protect, so she told Uncle Frank that she would tell Dad if he didn't shut up; we got out of there as fast as we could. Then Rose told me that Uncle Frank was a liar cause Mom said he was. Uncle Frank left the next morning.

Maude's family in Sturgis, S.D., in 1928. Back row, left to right: Myrtle, 26; Fred, 24; Elmer, 20; Elsie, 22. Front row, left to right: Ruth, 12; Fred William Hunt, 58; Maude Weir Hunt, 46; Rose, 15.

Several months later I told Dad what Frank had told us. He said, "well don't worry about it," but I wasn't one to be put off and I knew Dad had never lied to me, so I said, "I don't care one way or the other, but I would like to know if Mom is Calamity Jane's daughter." I'll never forget the look he gave me, but he said, "yes, she is, but you have to promise not to tell anyone, not even Rose," which I promised to do. This promise I have kept until a few years ago.

I remember the great Christmas we always had. No, we never had many toys or dolls; if we had a doll, Mom made it out of pieces and scraps, then embroidered faces on them and sewed buttons on for eyes. We had all kinds of reused buttons, so the eyes could be blue or brown, or even red or pink.

I remember one toy that was purchased from Sears and Roebuck. It was a tin piano about a foot high with a Negro man sitting at the key board. Another Negro was standing beside the piano playing a banjo; he had hinged legs, which danced every which way when the juice, which came from a small battery, was turned on. We all enjoyed it and used it for family entertainment. I don't remember what tune they played, but the piano man's arms and legs moved in time to the man that played the piano and jigged. It was a real treat. I also remember a small Teddy bear I got one year for Christmas. It wasn't really new, but it had been washed and repaired. It think it was Fred's or Elmer's at one time, but it was now my very own.

Dad and the boys went up a small creek nearby to get our winter's wood, and always a Christmas tree, usually a small one, that sat on a table in the living room. One time they brought home a large one that stood on the floor. Mom always saved every scrap of tinsel. We had candle holders which we had to put on the tree first, as they had to be put on with a clip. Mom always put those on or checked each one to be sure they were put there to stay. We usually didn't trim the tree until just a few days before, as we wanted it to stay green for the magic moment when we finally lit the candles on Christmas Eve. We had lots of ornaments from past years, new ones some of us made or a stray doll that was too fragile to play with any more. The tinsel we all put on last; every side had to be just so.

Christmas Eve finally came. The gifts had been laid at the base of the tree days before, wrapped in fancy paper, most from previous years which had been saved, and sometimes pressed with a cool flat iron. Mom would then lay out the small candles. We got to hand them to her as she carefully put them in the little holders, making sure nothing would touch the small flames. Now everyone was called in to watch as Mom carefully lit each candle. Oh, what a beautiful sight as the tree lit up the room. Mom would start to sing Silent Night; we all joined in, as the farm house seemed to almost burst with the Christmas song, so long ago but yet so real, as I realized what a wonderful mother we had, and what a great childhood we all had. When the candles were about two-thirds burnt, each was blown out. The magic was gone, but the joy stayed in our hearts as we knew we would have another magic moment next year.

Myrtle, the oldest, went to a teacher's college in Spearfish; she then taught school for several years. She was the caring one of the family. She would buy Rose and I dolls and nice sweaters, things that Mom and Dad couldn't afford. I remember she bought Elsie a chain with a fancy thing in front. Elsie thought it was great until they got into a fight and Elsie threw it at Myrtle. Elsie was always jealous of Myrtle as Myrtle was always small and Elsie was plump. We all called her Heavy. Myrtle was jealous of Elsie as Elsie had curly hair and could play all kinds of instruments, so when they met it was always an argument. Mom didn't side with either one, as she knew like the rest of us that Elsie was as ornery as her famous grandmother.

Myrtle married a country boy from White River where she was teaching school. His mother was dead, so his Dad lived with them, or they lived with him, I'm not sure, but that arrangement didn't last too long, as Myrtle and her husband Emmette moved out. They came to Dad's place, but Dad had no work for them, so they moved on up near Strool where they rented a farm. They adopted a small boy called Donny.

Emmette had a couple of hounds. The neighbors hired him and the hounds to kill coyotes that were killing their calves in the spring. There were hundreds of them, so Emmette bought a good saddle horse, one that could keep up with the hounds. I don't know how much they paid him, but the money sure helped them out as in those days a dime was a dime.

I'll never forget the time I went to see them. Emmette liked his jokes. He told me he wanted me to take his new horse and go get some cattle that were just over the hill. It was a new horse for me, so I gladly agreed to go as I always liked to try a new one. When I started to leave, those three mangy-looking hounds got up to go with me. As I was used to our cattle dog, I let them go along. We had just topped a hill and everything was great; the horse had lots of spirit and was an easy rider. The hounds ran on ahead. Then the horse exploded. I had a tight rein on him, but I hadn't expected this. He reared up on his hind legs and took off; then I saw what the trouble was. The hounds had spotted a jackrabbit across a little valley and on the other hill; they let a howl and took off in hot pursuit. The horse, of course, had been trained to follow, so over the hill and dale we went. I was pulling leather like I'd never pulled before, but I did stay on. After a wild and long ride, the hounds caught the rabbit and made it their supper. They found two more before we finally found the cattle that Emmette supposedly wanted me to bring in for him, but after the first one I knew what to expect. When we got back, of course Emmette was sitting on the wood pile laughing his head off, as he didn't want the cattle. He just wanted supper for his hounds. Wherever Emmette was, there were always jokes.

Elsie and Emmette were always playing jokes on one another. One time stands out, and even Dad laughed. Mom had cooked us all a nice dinner and Myrtle and Emmette were there for a visit. Emmette was helping Mom put the food on the table, and the rest of us were seated. The spice cupboard was just above the long cabinet. Emmette had his back to the table. He shyly reached up and got the Red pepper; he sprinkled it on a large slice of watermelon, and being it was red as the melon it didn't show much. Then he made a big mistake. He handed the first slice to Elsie. She knew right away something was wrong as we always served the closest one the first slice, and she was on the other side of the table. As Emmette was getting another slice, Elsie took a close look at the melon and she could see the red pepper on it. She didn't say anything, she just waited for Emmette to sit down with his slice. When he got seated, Elsie calmly picked up the slice of melon, came around to the other side where Emmette sat, and she slammed it down over Emmette's curly head. We all howled, and even Dad's eyes twinkled.Myrtle and Emmette Quatier lived in that part of the country for years. They traveled in a trailer house on vacations after they bought a small farm.

They would visit us all, usually with other people who also traveled in campers. They visited lots of places. They then sold the farm and bought a larger trailer house. They stayed in New Mexico for several years, then on to Wickenburg, Arizona. They stayed in a park and traveled in a smaller trailer in the summer time. This they really enjoyed. They were married for seventy years, and then Emmette died suddenly a few months later. Myrtle died recently, July 7, 1995, at age 93, a great lady.

Fred and Mary were married in 1923 when Fred was just 19 and I think Mary was 17 or 18. They tried farming, but times on farms were rough, so Fred got a job at the Homestake mine cutting timbers for the mine and then as a mechanic working on the machinery. Fred always had a job and was always a cheerful man. They raised eight children. I knew four of them, but after I moved to Idaho, I didn't see much of the other four.

They moved to Vale, South Dakota, where they had a filling station and a repair shop. Mary was always there to help. She got so she could repair cars too. Fred died in 1985 and Mary stayed in Vale. she was still planting a garden, although she could hardly walk. I think I can remember what their kids names were: Gertrude, Albert, Bobby, Marie, Bill, Jim, Helen, and Dorothy. He had thirty-one grandchildren and sixty-seven great-grandchildren.

Elsie married George Jeffery, who lived with his uncle on a big cattle ranch about twenty miles from us. They were married at the farm. After the wedding, Dad shook hands with

George and said, "I hope you know how to drive mules, cause you just married one." Everybody laughed. George proved himself over the years. We all liked him; he was hard-working and I liked him as well as I did my own brothers.

They lived for a while on the uncle's ranch, then they bought a farm of their own out near Vale. Elsie would come over and visit and one day she got a job playing the violin with another couple for a barn dance. They made about three dollars a night once a week. She wanted Rose to sing songs to her so she could listen to them; she could play anything she heard. Rose had a guitar that she played as she sang. Elsie played with the group for a few weeks, then she came home one day and said she was tired of just playing three or four tunes over and over all night. Then she looked at me and asked me why I didn't learn to play something. Years before, Myrtle wanted to give me music lessons on the piano, but when we tried to get Mom's piano tuned, the man told us it had gotten wet in it's many travels and the strings were all rusty, so that was the end of that as nobody had that kind of money. I had given up, as that was what I wanted to play. Elsie also owned a banjo mandolin that she played at the movie theater when they needed background music for the silent movies. So she tuned it up and told me to play it. She showed me how and where to put my fingers for a tune; it was, "Does Your Spearmint Lose Its Flavor on the Bed Post over Night." It seemed easy, and I got so I could pick out my own tunes as we had always sang songs together. Rose was there to help me as she listened to the radio, and when we heard a song we liked, we would each grab a pencil to get the words. I could always get the tune. It didn't take long for us to start up a string band. Elsie knew a drummer, Frankie Meyers; he could really make a drum talk, as long as he had a few drinks, but not too many. We played for barn dances and parties. We were called The Happy Four. It was lots of fun. Mom and Dad of course had to listen to the noise, but they never complained. We didn't get paid much, but we could at least buy a few yards of material for our dresses.

Elsie and George had to move off the farm as the drought hit their farm too. George went driving logging trucks. Elmer was busy with a job bringing in whisky from Canada for a man who didn't let the drivers know what they were hauling, but Elmer and I decided to look. We tried the wares, but I didn't like the taste. It didn't taste as good as Dad's home brew or Mom's chokecherry wine that I had sampled several times, but I darn near didn't get up the cellar steps.

It was hard times; there was no work of any kind. We had a few chickens. The grasshoppers got so thick that we started raising turkeys, as many as we could, mainly for self-defense as the turkeys kept them at least out of the front yard. Our wells went completely dry, but a neighbor drilled himself an artesian well. He found out there was an artesian basin under that part of the country. It was a big well, and he wanted to drill one for Dad as he said it showed water there too, but by that time Dad was too old to farm and he didn't have the money. I was the only one left. The neighbor told us we could drive what few cows we had over to his place to drink, which I gladly did. He also let us have all the water we needed, which we hauled with barrels on a wagon.

Rose married Orville Eveleth, a boy friend she had gone with for several years, and they moved to the state of Washington. It was lonesome, but yet a feeling of relief as she still bossed me and tried to make me act like a lady. But I was different and liked to do things one my own, so it seemed kinda like I was out of prison, but I didn't know what to do now that I was without her. I had only two years of high school, as we had no money to board me at Sturgis. The roads in the winter time were always drifted full of snow, so there was no way I could go to school. It was too cold to take a horse. I guess I could have married my boy friend, but he didn't have anything either, and something told me to just take off, but where?

Elsie came down from Custer and wanted me to come and stay with her as George had to be gone most of the time hauling gravel. He was gone for weeks at a time. While I was up there, I saw a sign of a beauty school. We were a couple miles out of town where they had rented a shack, so I went to the school to see if I could work my way through school. I really didn't like women that much, but I did like to cut hair, as Rose and I had always cut one another's, Mom's and Dad's, and anyone else's if they sat still long enough. The closest barber school was somewhere in North Dakota and it would cost too much for room and board. I went home and told Mom about the beauty school in Custer; she asked me if I wanted to go. I told her the school wanted $85 and I didn't have that much. She said she had sold a piece of land in Pierre and she would loan me the money. Mom was always there for us, so I borrowed it and went up to stay with Elsie and George at Custer.

School was a snap for me, and getting my room and board was a big help. I graduated the next spring.

I met my first husband when Elsie and I were playing at a party around a bonfire. Elsie liked her violin the best, and I learned to play a tenor banjo which I had bought several years before from a catalog where they sold rejects. I bought it for eleven dollars. It was perfect except the finger board wasn't set just right; the A-string had to be awfully tight in order to get a perfect tone. It sometimes snapped a string, but I played it for a long time and still have it.

I worked in Sturgis for Lola Felton for three or four years. It was a happy day when I paid Mom back the money she had lent me.

Elmer married a girl, Mavis Verene, who lived in a surrounding neighborhood. They had five kids. One of the boys got run over when he was about six. It was very sad. As he was running home to get his mittens, the road was very slick; the driver couldn't stop and the boy couldn't either. There were three boys and a girl left.

Elmer got a job repairing heavy-duty tractors and machinery. He lived in Custer, the same town where George was hauling logs. Their life wasn't always pleasant as Elmer turned into an alcoholic. Mavis stood by him, but it was hard. I saw a lot of him when I went to beauty school up at Custer. He was always a great favorite of mine as we both loved to dance. We had worn out the rugs in the old farm house doing the Charleston. The round dance hall up in Custer was our favorite place to dance. Everybody thought I was a girl friend instead of just his little sister.

He still had a motorcycle and I loved to ride with him. He liked to drink beer, but one glass was enough for me, so as a rule I could keep him almost sober. I had ridden with him on his motorcycle in the first motorcycle parade that Sturgis ever had. We then didn't realize how famous the races were to become years later. Elmer also played a famous character in the Days of 76 up at Deadwood.

Elmer was a good mechanic and could always get a job. Mavis, his wife, worked at a rock shop where they sold rocks to tourists, as the Hills had lots of beautiful rocks and minerals. She worked very hard trying to keep the kids fed and off the streets. She couldn't understand why Elmer loved to dance and party. I could as I was kinda the same type, but I didn't drink much. I was too busy trying to keep him sober.

After I graduated from the beauty school and went home to Sturgis, little brother didn't have anyone to play with. I felt so sorry for him and his family, but I didn't know what to do as he was as bull-headed as I was. There was no A.A.. then in our part of the country for him, so he was like his famous Grandmother and died an alcoholic. I will always feel guilty about it, as I was his little sister who adored him.

I never knew his kids very well as they were almost babies when I left. Doris, the oldest, is a real nice gal. His middle boy, Ray, is a favorite of mine. He doesn't look like his Dad, but he acts like him. I didn't know his first wife, but his second wife is a very special person. The other two boys I hardly know, but they say they are nice guys. After Elmer's death, Mavis held her family together. Then she remarried to a great guy; they had only a few short happy years together before his death. She is still living near her children in Arizona.

Rose was the tallest of us girls. She was very popular, and the only one who graduated from high school at Sturgis. She stayed on the farm most of the time, although she worked for several different people. Everybody depended on Rose, even if I didn't like it whenever she would pull me out of trouble. She never could understand that doing things was fun. Our Dad called her Grandma, as she was always worrying about what I would do next. She had a great sense of humor; we could sit and giggle about nothing. She always told me how to do everything; even if I had done it many times before, she would explain it all out in detail.

She was a very good dancer. She played the guitar, and sang western songs. She could also yodel, although she couldn't howl in the back of her throat like her famous Grandmother and her mother. Mom would try and show her how, but she couldn't give out that trill howl that could be heard for a mile or more.

Rose went with a guy who worked at one of the ranches, Orville Eveleth. He was Rose's type, never doing anything he shouldn't. In other words, no fun. He was a beautiful dancer, and they made an outstanding-looking couple on the dance floor.

Rose and Orville had two children, a boy Russell and a girl Rosalie. They are both grown and have grown kids of their own. Russell is a logging truck driver and Rosalie a hairdresser. Orville died of cancer a few months after their 50th wedding anniversary in Arizona. Rose carried on real good; she spends the winters in Arizona, then goes back to Graham, Washington, in the summer where she digs in her garden and flowers. She loves bowling and card-playing, and spends many hours at it. She is a great cook and is noted for her apple crisp. Orville never liked to fish, so they didn't go fishing. Now she and one of her neighbors, who used to live just across the road from her, go fishing in Alaska, although she is 83. I'm real proud of her.

RUTH'S STORY

I am Ruth, the youngest, and the most like her Grandmother. I always had somebody making me mind and keeping me out of trouble, even if I was hard-headed. I was always very shy. I used to run and hide behind the bed, which was a solid head-board and high enough for me to hide behind, when anyone came to visit. Most people thought there were only five of us, until I had to go to school. I started for a few months when I was five. I remember the first day of school. There were three of us in the first grade. We were only a few months apart. There was Earl Matz, Alma Hooper, and myself. We were let out to play in the playground ahead of the rest. I forget what Earl and I got to arguing about, but we got into a fight. I wrestled him to the ground, and when the teacher came out I was astride him and was slapping his face first on one side and then the other. The teacher made us come inside and she wouldn't let us go home until we apologized to one another. That was hard to do, as I thought he was in the wrong, but I didn't want to walk home alone and I hated to face my Mother as I knew from the others that Mom always took the teacher's side. So I knew my Mother would be waiting for me; she just looked at me; she then told me she wanted no more fighting, and you can bet there wasn't any.

School was fun. We usually had the best of teachers. We played baseball, usually with a board for a bat, and a sponge rubber ball. Other times we played tag, or something that everyone could play, and something that didn't take any money for supplies. The school board always supplied us with books and large maps; somebody donated a large dictionary which was laid on a small desk in the back of the one room where everyone could go back and use it.

Another one of our games we called shinny. All we needed was a tin can and a stick of some shape or form. It was the wildest of games. We would hit the can trying to get it to a goal which was a mark we scratched into the ground. We had about 40 feet in between the goals. Of course we gave it our all, so we fell a lot and the knees of my stockings were always torn. I really didn't mind, but my mother didn't care about the game; she got tired mending and warned me about it to no avail, so she told me to stop playing the game, as from now on I would have to mend my own stockings. This was hard to take and I knew she always had an answer to anything, and I didn't like to mend stockings as they didn't look like Mom's neat mends. I had to think fast on that one, so I rolled down my stockings before we started playing. Whether she knew what I did or not, I'm not sure, but I sure went to our room in a hurry to get on my overalls so she wouldn't see the scrapes.

We of course didn't have buses, so when it was time to go to high school, Rose batches with Hazel Matz, one of the neighborhood girls, for three years, then I batched with Rose on her last year. Dad rented a room which had a small stove and a bed. I liked that real well, but Rose had only the one year left, so the next year Dad found me a place to board if I helped with the house work, which I did of one year. Somehow the lady and I didn't click. All I went was the two years. I loved school, but times were getting worse. Although I loved basketball, I was a teenager and didn't think is was worth the effort. Anyway, I liked the farm best, even if it was drying up. We couldn't take typing until we were seniors, as they didn't have enough typewriters, and that's what I wanted to learn.

Shortly after that, Elsie said she needed someone to help her make up a band, and I was elected. That was very interesting and we were out with the crowds, which I really liked as long as they kept their distance. Then Elsie and Rose left. I was on my own again. Elsie again came to my rescue when she wanted me to come and stay with her and go to beauty school. I wished it was a barber school, but the closest one was in North Dakota.

I worked in a beauty shop in Sturgis for several years, giving permanents and cutting hair. Then I married Munroe Kouba, who cut logs. We lived in logging camps for about a year, then he went to work mining mica in an open mine. They mined feldspar and mica. I loved the large sheets of mica; it was so beautiful. It was quite a sight to see it roll out of the feldspar in large chunks as they blasted the rock. A company in South Carolina wanted it split in thin pieces. This we could do with sharp knives. Some pieces would cover the bottom of a powder box. At that time they used these pieces in toasters, irons, and other appliances. The men mined it, and us women split and trimmed it.

My husband worked at several mines in the Black Hills. I'll never forget the time he worked at a mine near Keystone. We could see Mount Rushmore from where we lived; they were carving it at this time.. It was real nice to look up each morning and see what had changed. Then one morning I looked up and Washington's nose had slid off; he looked a little bald-faced. We later heard they had to drill back into the mountain in order to make him another nose. It changed the position of his face, but they did a beautiful job.

We then moved to Wallace, Idaho, where my husband got a job at the Hecla silver and lead mine. I got a job in Bessie Brewer's beauty shop. I waited on the big bosses wives to the red light girls. Of course, the nice ladies didn't realize who they were sitting beside, but the girls knew who the ladies were. Of course, they knew the husbands better. I liked the girls; they tipped great and they kept Wallace safe at night; nobody had to be afraid to walk down the streets of Wallace. The girls stayed in their rooms, not out on the streets. I worked in the shop until I was eight months pregnant with our first boy, Lamont. I decided to stay home and take care of my own boys as I had another boy, Norman, three years later.

We stayed in Wallace until Norman was about three. Munroe wasn't feeling well, so we left the mines. He got a job as a powder man on the road they were making up the Locksaw River. It was quite an experience. It was almost a wilderness. We lived in a tent all summer, but the air was great, the fish were plentiful, and the boys had two dogs that knew the way home. It was a fun summer; the huckleberries were huge and juicy. Of course, we had to watch out for the brown bears who loved the berries too, but we had a small dog that was a fox terrier and much to our surprise he loved to chase bears. If a bear got too close, we would tell him to get the bear. The bear would look at the little dog, the dog would bark and hold his ground until one of us would say, "get him Tyke," and the little dog would nip the bear on the heels. The bear would take a swing at the dog, but Tyke was too fast and the bear couldn't hit him. Then the bear would run off. All the crew would go with us to pick the berries, with the little dog close behind.

The doctors couldn't find out what to do with Munroe as he had a bad valve in his heart. He died in 1957. We lived in Boise in a trailer house, usually in a court, until Lamont found a piece of land we could buy in Garden City. It was a good place as the kids had some freedom. A friend of ours bought half the land and moved us and himself onto the land. We got Social Security for the boys and myself which was a great help. I went to the State Board for a license, but they would not give me one unless I went back to school and took their State Board. They would not honor my Manager's License from South Dakota. I felt like blowing my stack as I had already worked in Wallace. I just told them to go jump in the lake, and I went to work cleaning houses. I worked for one person for one day each week; as a rule, I found them very nice. Once in a while I stayed only a few hours, but some I worked for years.

A woman I met wanted me to take a job with her waiting tables at a dance hall. I told her that I had never waited tables; she said I couldn't learn any younger, so I went with her on Saturday nights. They called it the Mirra Mar. They brought in large bands such as the Royal Canadians, the Waltz King who was the greatest of the saxophone players and was the nicest of them all. They also had Louis Armstrong who in my opinion had his other trumpet player play the high notes while he mopped his brow and took credit for it. It was there I met my second husband. He tended bar on Saturday night but worked as a carpenter in the daytime. He was a sad-looking man. He had just gotten a divorce; his ex-wife got everything they had, including his two boys. We've been married for thirty-four years. I believe I married the two best men that ever was. His name is Miles Shadley, but we all call him Lee.

Mom and Dad

Mom and Dad stayed on the farm. They had sold most everything. Dad didn't feel good and was getting older. We had all scattered, and the farm was still too dry, so the neighbor who drilled the wells bought it as he still thought he could get lost of water, and he did.

Mom and Dad moved into Sturgis where they celebrated their 50th wedding anniversary. We all got together for the first time in many years. I guess they set the scene, as Myrtle and Emmettte were married for 70 years; Fred and Mary for 62 years; Elsie and George for 52 years; Elmer and Mavis for about 47 years; and Rose and Orville for 50 years a few months before his death. My first husband died after we were married 18 years. I married Miles Shadley and we have been married for 34 years. They must have raised us right or maybe we just picked out good mates who put up with us.

Years later Mom had several strokes. Elsie lived just outside of Sturgis. When she called me, I knew Elsie got frightened real easy so I called to see how Mom was. As I was living in Idaho and it was mighty cold, I knew it was even colder in South Dakota. It was zero, but Mom was no better so my husband put me on a plane and Elsie's husband came to Rapid City to get me. George said Mom was no better and she was in a coma. He said the doctor said she couldn't last long. When we got to their farm, Elsie was very upset and she thought we should go to Deadwood to stay, at least her and I as George had to take care of their cattle. George took up their camper, a big one he had made to go fishing in. We went in to see Mom and she looked real peaceful as if she was sleeping. I talked to her and to everyone's surprise, she patted my hand. That gave us hope, but a week later she died, never fully regaining consciousness. Elsie couldn't grasp the fact that she was gone, so I stayed until after the funeral. Mom had most of her things at Elsie's place, and I could see Elsie wasn't ready to go through Mom's things. I told her I'd better head for home to my husband and boys. Elsie asked me what I wanted of Mom's things, and I told her Mom had given me my share already, so divide it up amongst the others and to not worry about it for a while.

The next spring, Elsie and George decided to go to Rose's home, which was near Tacoma, Washington. It was there that Elsie finally broke down and told Rose that while looking through Mom's papers, she found Mom's birth certificate, and like Uncle Frank said, she was Calamity Jane's daughter. Elsie kept asking Rose what she should do with it. Rose could see Elsie was really upset about it, so she told her to do whatever she wanted to do. Rose did not see it, and nobody knows what she did with it. Later, Rose and I have asked her about it, but she just looks off into space with a set look on her face.

When her husband, George, died and we put Elsie into a nursing home years later, it was not in the safety box, although Mom's adoption papers are. Rose told me what Elsie said years later. I told her I'd known it for years. When she told Elmer, he said he had worked on some heavy duty equipment in Pierre where he met an old man who asked him if he was one of Maud's boys; when Elmer said he was, the old man told him that he had known our mother, and he knew she was Calamity Jane's daughter. Fred knew about it before he left Pierre, but didn't want Mom to know he knew it. Myrtle had heard about it before they left Pierre, so she asked Mom about it, and Mom told her not to ask such foolish questions, and that settled the matter. Rose, Elsie, and Myrtle were the only ones that didn't know for sure.

My Thoughts About the Movie "Buffalo Girls"

I think Anjelica Huston played the part of Calamity Jane very well, but the writer couldn't get the dates right. Nothing jived. We all know Wild Bill Hickok was shot August 2, 1876, by Jack McCall; all of our history books told us that. This has been proven over and over again. In other words, Calamity's child was born before that. According to Calamity, the baby she was supposed to have had was born in 1873; that was three years before Wild Bill was shot. History also has it that Annie Oakley, who was noted for her shooting, went with Buffalo Bill when he went to England. The only time he went to England, which was in 1887, Calamity Jane, so the story went, went with him and there saw her daughter, or should we say her so-called daughter, who looked to me as if she was 6 or 7. Now comes the dates: the daughter would of been at least 14, anyway that's the way I was taught to subtract.

Calamity in her later days confessed she lied to everybody because she thought it was fun. The history books said she did star with Buffalo Bill in his Wild West Show when he took his troupe to the eastern states; it also told she was a great success, until she got too drunk to ride or shoot, so he fired her.

They made another error when they let you think, at least, that Dora Dufran died when she had a baby. I'm sure most of you knew that Dora Dufran didn't die until August 5, 1934. I was in Sturgis at the time.

Long Jo's old violin with the beautiful tone, that Elsie later played.

This is the old sandstone barn that still stands on our old farm. I've never seen one like it, the sandstone is cut in blocks, we think they got the sandstone from a mountain which is a few miles away on Fort Meade Reservation, years before we moved in, in 1915. There is a wooden garage on one side. Dad built a large wooden cow barn on the east side.

The man who now owns the barn says it is crumbling badly on the south side; he tried to have it repaired as a historical marker, but so far no luck.